Table of Contents

I0016957

- Optimize your URLs for SEO
4. Title and Description Tags Optimization
   - Front-load Title tag
   - Use Title tag modifiers
   - Use Unique, Keyword-Rich Meta Descriptions
5. Search Engine Optimized Content Writing
   - Unique Content
   - Valuable Content
   - Contents that satisfies Search Intent
6. Optimization for CTR
   - Use "Question Title Tags"
   - Fill in Missing Meta Descriptions
   - Use Review or FAQ Schema
   - Add some emotion to Title tags
   - Add the current year to Title and Description
7. On-Page UX Signals
   - Push Content above the Fold
   - Chunk your Content
   - Engage an Active Community
8. Advanced On-Page SEO Tips
   - Use Original Images
   - Do internal Linking
   - Write Comprehensive Content
   - Boost your Page Speed
   - Image Optimization
   - Rank your Content in Featured Snippets

Chapter 3: Off-Page SEO
1. On-Page SEO v/s Off-Page SEO
2. Boost Off-Page SEO with Backlinks
   - Be a Data Source
   - Double Down on Long-Form Content
   - Strategic Guest Posting
3. Generate Brand Signals
4. Improve E-A-T
   - Get Brand Mentions on Authority Sites
   - Get Links from Trusted "Seed Sites"
   - Get Positive Reviews Online

Chapter 4: Technical SEO
1. How to improve Technical SEO?
2. Site Structure and Navigation
   - Use a Flat, Organized Site Structure
   - Consistent URL Structure

- Breadcrumbs Navigation
3. Crawling, Rendering and Indexing
    - Spot Indexing Issues
        1) Coverage Report
        2) Screaming Frog
        3) Ahrefs Site Audit
        4) Internal Link to "Deep" Pages
        5) Use an XML Sitemap
        6) GSC "Inspect"
4. Thin and Duplicate Content
    - Use Canonical URLs
5. PageSpeed
    - Reduce Web Page Size
    - Test Load Times with and without a CDN
    - Eliminate 3rd Party Scripts

Chapter 5: Country-Specific SEO
1. How to target a specific country?
2. Website Structure choices for Internal SEO
    - CCTLDs
    - Sub-Domains
    - Sub-Directories
3. Technical Signals for Internal SEO
    1. HrefLang Tags
    2. Canonical Tags
    3. X Default Tags
    4. Meta Content Language Tags
    5. Schema Markup
4. Create a Sitemap
5. Change content based on local culture
6. International Link Building

Chapter 6: Google's 8 Most Important Ranking Factors (2021)

Chapter 7: Bonus: SEO in 2021
1. Core Web Vitals
    - Largest Contentful Paint (LCP)
    - First Input Delay (FID)
    - Cumulative Layout Shift (CLS)
2. Google Passages Ranking
    - How to Opimize for Passages?
3. Featured Snippets
    - How to Optimize for Featured Snippets?
4. Visual Search

Search Engine Optimization (SEO): An Overview

Search Engine Optimization, as the name indicates, consists of 3 fundamentals:

1. The Search

Search refers to the words that people write to find what they are looking for with their intent of finding. E.g. if one searches for Search Engine Optimization with the intent to only know what it means, might search it as "Search Engine Optimization definition" where the word definition refers to the intent of mere introduction of the word Search Engine Optimization, but if one searches for Search Engine Optimization with the intent to understand the whole process for ranking his website might search it as "How to do Search Engine Optimization complete guide" where "how to do" and "complete guide" refers to the intent of understanding the complete process.

2. The Engine for Search

The Engine for Search or the "Search Engine" is the place where people search online to find what they are looking for. e.g. Google, Bing, Yahoo, etc.
Search Engines were created to help users locate the most relevant information based on their search queries and are an integral part of the World Wide Web. Google's search methodology paved the way for relevant search and was key to the rise of search engines on the web. Other search engines such as Yahoo!, Bing, Baidu, and Yandex have joined the fray as competition to Google.

3. The Optimization concerning the Search with respect to the particular Engine for Search

"Optimization" here is in reference to the process of making your content compatible with what the people/users are searching for in the Search Engines. This process requires a deep dive into the understanding of the particular Search Engine as the search engine crawls on the data online and finds the most relevant results to the search and the searcher's intent. So, along with numerous other ranking factors, the particular search engine ranks some certain websites higher than the others.
Hence, optimization is the process of due diligence for ranking higher in results of a search on a search engine.

So, what is needed to understand is that Search Engine Optimization requires a good understanding of all the 3 fundamentals present in its name. Now, it will be explained step by step.

❖ What is Search Engine Optimization (SEO)?

Search Engine Optimization (SEO) is the practice of continually optimizing a website in order to rank in the organic, non-paid search engine results pages (SERPs).
SEO is often about making small modifications to parts of the website. When viewed individually, these changes might seem like incremental improvements, but when combined with other optimizations, they could have a noticeable impact on the site's user experience and performance in organic search results. Common tasks associated with SEO include creating high-quality content, optimizing content around specific keywords, and building backlinks.

❖ Types of Search Engine Optimization (SEO):

- On-page SEO
- Off-page SEO
- Technical SEO
- User Interaction Signals

1. On-Page SEO:

On-Page SEO is the optimization of one's website around keywords that one's target customer searches for in search engines. For example, one on-page SEO best practice is to include the main keyword in one's title tag, meta description and webpage URL.

2. Off-Page SEO:

Off-page SEO is all about getting trust and authority signals from other websites. This mainly involves building high-quality backlinks to one's site.

3. Technical SEO:

Google and other search engines can crawl and index all the pages on one's website. Technical SEO also includes things like making sure one's pages load quickly. And that one's site architecture is set up correctly.

4. User Interaction Signals:

The way that users interact with one's site helps Google figure out if one's page is a good match for someone's search. For example, if one's page has a high bounce rate, that could be a sign that the page isn't giving someone the answer to their query. And if Google considers one's page a bad fit for that keyword, it can drop one's rankings down a bit or completely off of the first page altogether.

❖ How does Search Engine work?

To understand, Google as an example would be best. When one searches for something in Google (or any other search engine), an algorithm works in real-time to bring what that search engine considers the "best" result.

Specifically, Google scans its index of hundreds of billions of pages to find a set of results that will best answer one's search.

❖ How does Search Engine Optimization work?

SEO works by optimizing one's site for the search engine that one wants to rank for, whether it's Google, Bing, Amazon or YouTube. Specifically, the job is to make sure that a search engine sees one's site as the overall best result for a person's search.

How they determine the "best" result is based on an algorithm that takes into account authority, relevancy to that query, loading speed, and more (For example, Google has over 200 ranking factors in their algorithm).

❖ Difference between Organic vs. Paid Results

Search engine result pages are separated into two distinct sections: organic and paid results.

1. Organic Search Results

Organic search results (sometimes referred to as "natural" results) are natural results that rank based 100% on merit. In other words, there's no way to pay Google or other search engines in order to rank higher in the organic search results.

Search engines rank organic search results based on hundreds of different ranking factors. But in general, organic results are deemed by Google to be the most relative, trustworthy, and authoritative websites or web pages on the subject.

The important thing to keep in mind is that when "SEO" is discussed, it is about ranking your website higher up in the organic search results not in the paid search results.

1. Paid Results

Paid search results are ads that appear on top of or underneath the organic results.

Paid ads are completely independent of the organic listings. Advertisers in the paid results section are "ranked" by how much they are willing to pay for a single visitor from a particular set of search results (known as "Pay Per Click Advertising").

❖ How does Google determine the "best" result?

Even though Google doesn't make the inner workings of its algorithm public, based on filed patents and statements from Google, it is known that websites and web pages are ranked based on some ranking factors such as:

1. Relevance

Google looks first-and-foremost for pages that are closely related to the searcher's keyword. However, Google doesn't simply rank "the most relevant pages at the top". That's because there are thousands (or even millions) of relevant pages for every search term. For example, the keyword "burger recipe" brings up 778 million results in Google.
So, in order to filter the best to the top, Google relies on other elements of its algorithm too.

2. Authoritativeness

Google determines the content is accurate and trustworthy by looking at the number of other pages that link to that page (which is called "backlinking"). Generally, the more links a page has, the higher it ranks.
Google is different from other search engines due to this "backlinking" measurement factor, as other search engines lack it.

3. Usefulness

Google prefers an organized in discrete sections kind of content written by a layman over unorganized content by an expert of the field. Content that is easy to understand by the users enhancing the User Experience Signals because it is organized in distinct sections will be preferred by Google.

❖ Why is SEO important?

Search Engine Optimization (SEO) is important because search is a BIG source of traffic. In fact, here's a breakdown of where most website traffic originates:

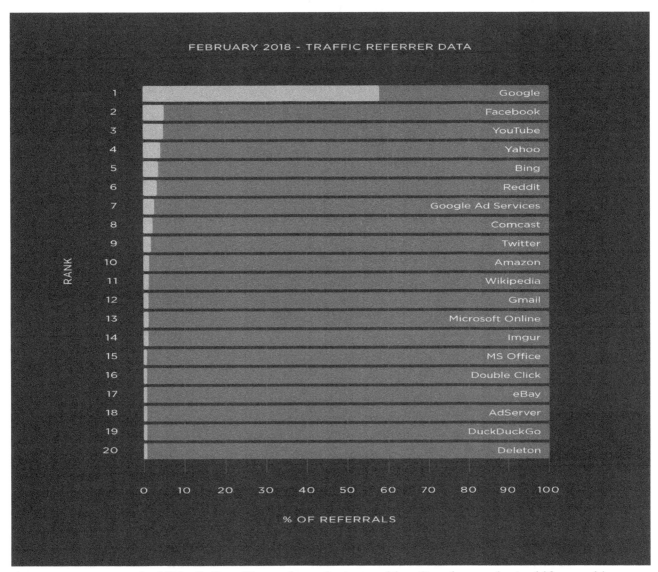

FEBRUARY 2018 - TRAFFIC REFERRER DATA

As you can see, nearly 60% of all traffic on the web starts with a Google search. And if you add together traffic from other popular search engines (like Bing, Yahoo, and YouTube), 70.6% of all traffic originates from a search engine.

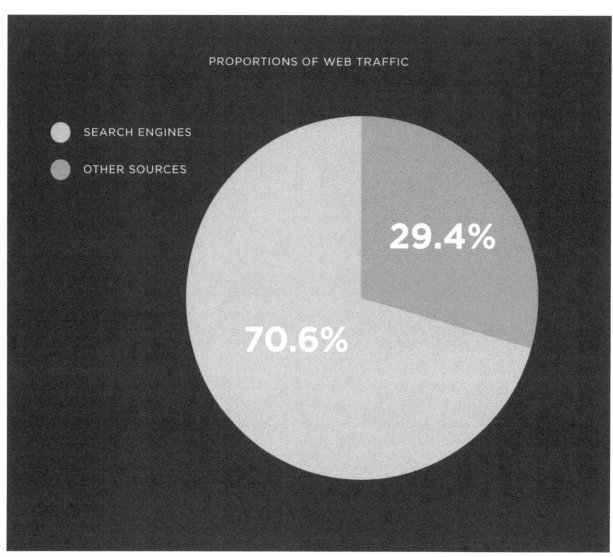

For example, let's say that one runs a party supply company. According to the Google Keyword Planner, 110,000 people search for "party supplies" every single month.

Considering that the first result in Google gets around 20% of all clicks, that's 22,000 visitors to one's website each month if one show up at the top.

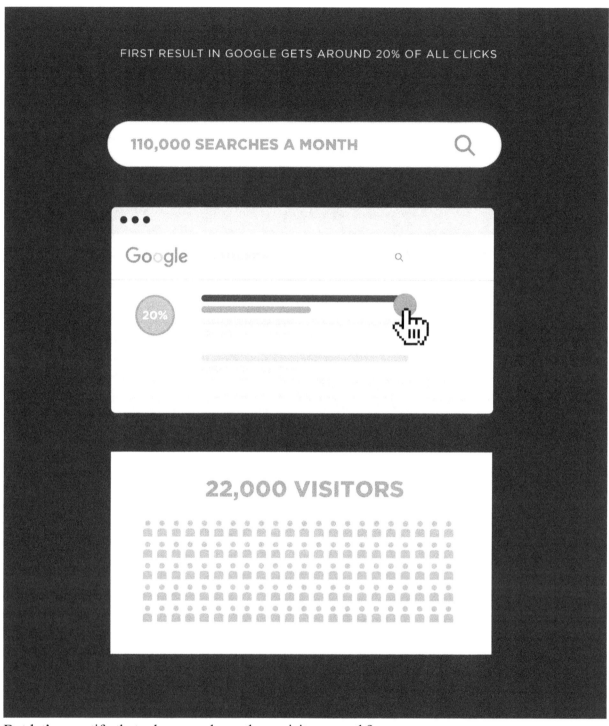

But let's quantify that – how much are those visitors worth?

The average advertiser for that search phrase spends about 1 dollar per click which means that the web traffic of 22,000 visitors is worth roughly $22,000 a month.

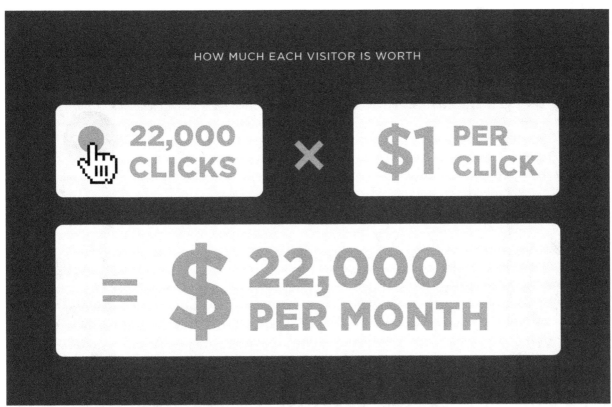

And that's just for that search phrase. If one's site is SEO-friendly, then one can rank for hundreds (and sometimes thousands) of different keywords. In other industries, like real estate or insurance, the value of search engine traffic is significantly higher. For example, advertisers are paying over $45 per click on the search phrase "auto insurance price quotes".

SEARCH ENGINE TRAFFIC VALUE VARIES ACROSS INDUSTRIES

How to do Search Engine Optimization (SEO)?

❖ Customers and Keywords

Before Technical SEO (Title tags, Href tags and Html etc.) an important step is Customer and Keyword Research which is where it can be figured out what are the exact words and phrases with which the people/users/customers search for in the search engine. After finding that out, one can use it to rank the site in the organic SERPs.

❖ How to do it? What are the steps?

1. Customer Research

The first step is to develop a Customer Persona which means what are the details of your targetted customer. For example,

Persona: High School Basketball Player Parent

Age 37 - 59

Gender Male or Female

Approximate Income
$50,000 - $150,000 per year

Hobbies & Interests: Celtics fan, playing pickup basketball, spending time with son or daughter.

Things they struggle with: Having more free time to exercise and spend time with kids (hence the desire for a basketball hoop).

Goals: Son or daughter to play college basketball for Division I or II school.

Customer research by Customer Persona is an integral part of the process as it not just helps out in finding what the people want but also super important for SEO and content marketing. What is meant is that to succeed with SEO, the need is in creating content around topics of customer desire (what they search for) and unless it is not known who or what kind of the customers are, it's very unlikely to understand the customer search.

HubSpot's Make My Persona is a free and good tool to create a detailed Customer Persona.

2. Keyword Research

Once you have a Customer Persona, the next step is Keyword Research where you figure out what are the exact words and phrases (search queries) that customers type into the search engine. The keywords can be Product Keywords or Informational Keywords, where the former refers to the keywords people use to find what one sells while the latter refers to the keywords that people use just for informational purpose when not looking to buy what one sells.

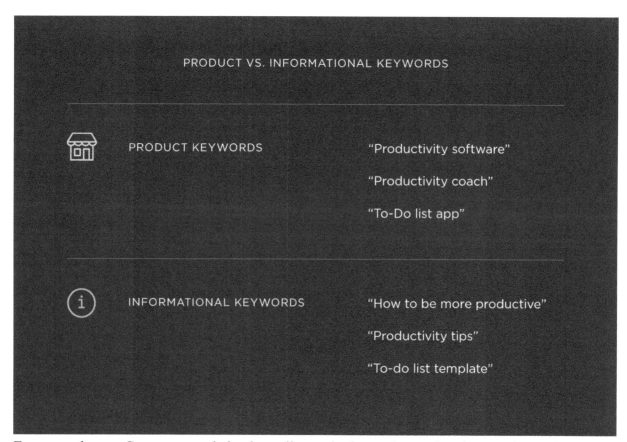

For example, an eCommerce website that sells tennis shoes, the product keywords would be like:

- Tennis shoes free shipping

- Nike tennis shoes

- Tennis shoes for flat feet

On the contrary, Informational Keywords are what audience is interested in when not necessarily searching for shoes:

- Second serve tutorial

- How to stop unforced errors

- Proper backhand form

- How to hit a topspin serve

To succeed with SEO, one needs to optimize pages on one's website around both types of keywords. So, when a customer searches for the product, one's site comes up in the search engine results and for keywords that the customers use when not looking for a product or service, even then one's site comes up for those too.

❖ Keyword Research Tips

Here are a few tips to help finding keywords.

1. Use Google Autocomplete

Whenever something is typed into Google, it provides a bunch of search suggestions. So, type keyword ideas into Google and write down any suggestions that comes up.

Google

paleo diet

paleo diet
paleo diet **foods**
paleo diet **recipes**
paleo diet **definition**
paleo diet **plan**
paleo diet **breakfast**
paleo diet **benefits**
paleo diet **macros**
paleo diet **results**
paleo diet **snacks**

Google Search   I'm Feeling Lucky

2. **Use** Answer The Public.

Answer The Public (ATP) is a great free tool to find the informational keywords that people are searching for. Write those keywords down and later use it on the site.

For example, if the site to be optimized is a blog about the Paleo Diet, then "paleo diet" is to be typed into ATP and it will pump out questions that people ask around that topic.

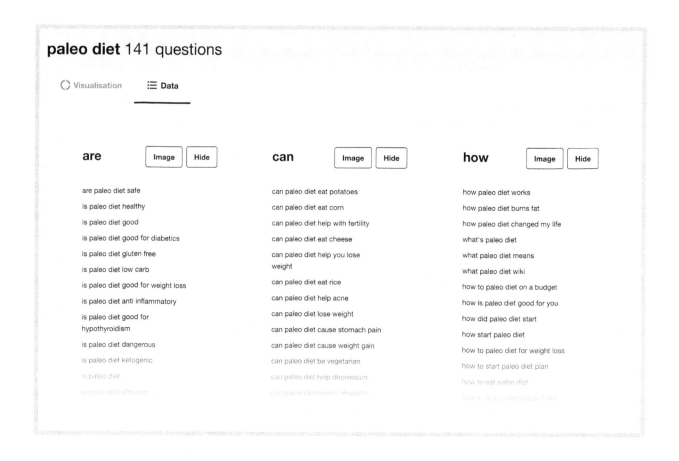

3. Use a Keyword Research Tool

Keyword Research Tools are the digital tools that helps in figuring out the frequency of search of a particular keyword (word or a phrase being searched) and the level of competition with other sites for that specific keyword to rank on the first page of Google. Simply put, a keyword research tool helps in choosing the best keywords with more frequent searches and less competition letting your site in achieving a higher rank in the SERPs. Namely, some good Keyword Research Tools are:

- Google's Keyword Planner (Google's free and handy to use tool)
- Moz Keyword Explorer (a perfect SEO Tool)
- SEMRush (a wonderful tool for SEO)
- MozBar (a Search Engine Extension of Moz)
- Keywords Everywhere Extension (a Search Engine Extension limited to few countries)

But the best all-around free keyword tool is Google's Keyword Planner.

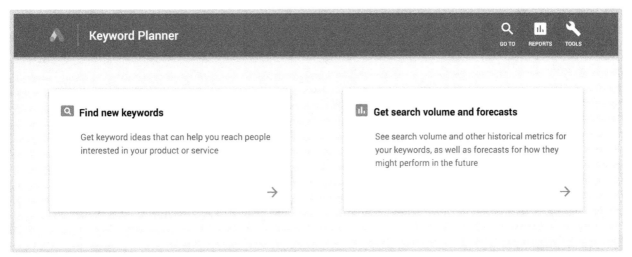

Even though Keyword Planner was designed to help people with Google Ads campaigns, it still helps in finding keywords for SEO. All one needs to do is to enter a product keyword or informational keyword into it.

Data on that exact phrase (like a search volume range) and a list of related keywords will appear right after.

Keyword (by relevance)	Avg. monthly searches	Competition	Ad impression share	Top of page bid (low range)	Top of page bid (high range)
Your search term					
paleo diet	100K – 1M	Low	–	$0.05	$0.53
Idea					
paleo	10K – 100K	Low	–	$0.53	$8.02
paleo recipes	10K – 100K	Low	–	$0.54	$2.60
paleo diet plan	1K – 10K	Medium	–	$0.84	$3.33
paleo diet foods	1K – 10K	Low	–	$0.08	$1.98
the paleo diet	1K – 10K	Low	–	$0.07	$0.40
paleo foods	1K – 10K	High	–	$0.47	$2.59
paleo cookbook	1K – 10K	High	–	$0.32	$0.68
paleo diet food list	1K – 10K	Low	–	$0.07	$2.14
paleo diet recipes	1K – 10K	Medium	–	$0.50	$2.29
paleo diet book	100 – 1K	High		$0.32	$0.67

The search volume range is just one problem in the free version as it doesn't show the exact number of searches but at least provides some idea of how many times that keyword gets searched for a specific period of time. For a more exact search volume data, a Google Ads campaign is to be run.

A 3rd party tool (like Ahrefs, SEMRush, etc.) with a more precise search volume information can also be used. Generally, the ranges are not much of a pain as they at least give an idea which is helpful in figuring out the relative search volume between different keywords.

4. Use Google Trends

Monthly Search Volume is essential as it tells a lot about the Search Volume but not about how it is trending. Google Trends is a free tool that provides significant information on the keyword trends.

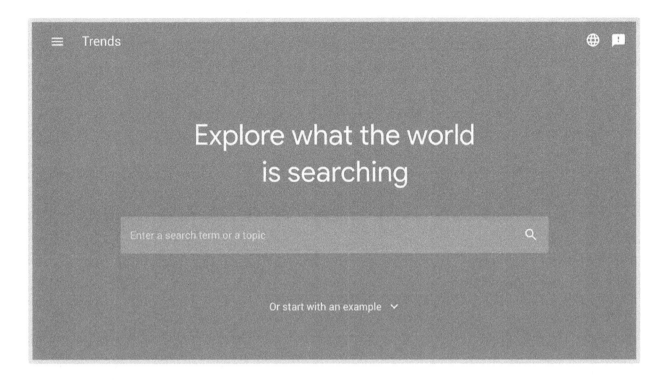

❖ **Types of Keywords:**

   1. Long-Tail Keywords
   2. Short-Tail Keywords

1. **Long-Tail Keywords:**

Long-tail keywords are those search terms that have relatively low search volume and competition levels. Moreover, long-tail terms tend to have longer lengths (3+ words) than other keyword types.

A beginner in SEO must focus on long-tail keywords as long-tail keywords have a lower competition but a higher conversion due to it.

Number of Keywords: Competition vs. Conversion

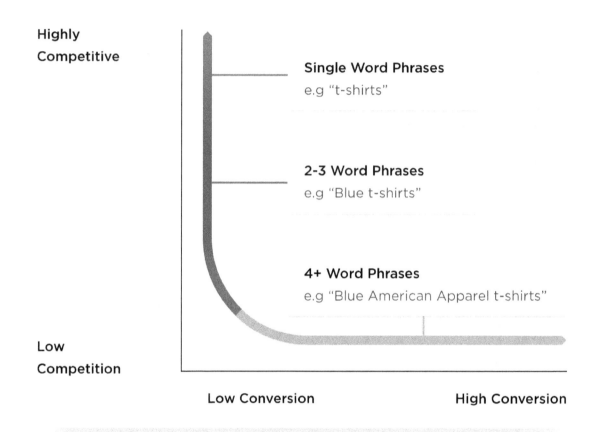

After getting a bit of experience in SEO, then one can start focusing and targeting short-tail keywords which are more competitive than the long-tail ones.

2. Short-Tail Keywords

Short-tail keywords are search terms that have a high search volume and competition levels. Furthermore, short-tail terms tend to have short lengths of no more than three words. Their spectrum consists of very broad topics rather than specific ones.

For example, "running shoes" is an example of a short tail keyword than that of "best running shoes for winter" which is an example of a long tail keyword.

On-Page SEO

On-Page SEO (also known as "on-site SEO") is the optimization of one's website around keywords that one's target customer searches for in search engines. For example, one on-page SEO best practice is to include the main keyword in one's title tags, meta descriptions, content, internal links and webpage URL.

❖ **On-Page SEO Essentials:**

On-page SEO (also known as "on-site SEO") is the practice of optimizing web page content for search engines and users. Common on-page SEO practices include optimizing title tags, content, internal links and URLs.

❖ **Importance of On-Page SEO:**

Google's own "How Search Works" report states that:

Relevance of webpages

Next, algorithms analyze the content of webpages to assess whether the page contains information that might be relevant to what you are looking for.

The most basic signal that information is relevant is when a webpage contains the same keywords as your search query. If those keywords appear on the page, or if they appear in the headings or body of the text, the information is more likely to be relevant. Beyond simple keyword matching, we use aggregated and anonymized interaction data to assess whether search results are relevant to queries. We transform that data into signals that help our machine-learned systems better estimate relevance.

So, this clearly portrays the importance of On-Page SEO as without it any page or won't rank much.

❖ **On-Page SEO Optimization:**

In 2021, steps should be taken for On-Page SEO Optimization to opimize the site or page to rank:

1. **Use Target Keyword In The First 100 Words** (Google puts more weight on terms that show up early in your page).

2. **Wrap Blog Post Title in an H1 Tag** (H1 tags help Google understand the structure of the page which helps Google to find the relevant content easily).

3. **Wrap Subheadings in H2 Tags** (Include a target keyword in at least one subheading).

4. **Keyword Frequency** (No. of times a keyword appears in one's content - Use it naturally rather than overstuffing it all over the content).

5. **Use External (Outbound) Links** (Help Google think your page as a source of quality information by attaching external links to related pages which also helps Google in figuring out your page's topic)

6. **Optimize Your URLs for SEO** (Make your URLs short and include a keyword in every URL).

❖ **Title and Description Tags Optimization**

1. **Front-load Title tag** (Put the Title Tag closer to the beginning - most important as it provides Google a high level overview of one's site/page).
2. **Use Title Tag Modifiers** (Using modifiers like "best", "good", "great", "guide", "checklist", "fast" and "review" can help in ranking for long tail versions of your target keyword).
3. **Use Unique, Keyword-Rich Meta Descriptions** (A good meta description helps one's result stand out, which can boost one's organic CTR).

❖ **Search Engine Optimized Content Writing**

1. **Unique Content** (Content that brings something new to the table).
2. **Valuable Content** (Add details, Crisp writing, Updated material, Expert authors, Delete "dead weight" pages).
3. **Content That Satisfies Search Intent** (The page has to be exactly what a Google searcher wants).

❖ **Optimization for CTR**

Click-Through Rate (CTR) is very important as it is one of the Google Ranking Factors. The following steps should be taken to use it to support website's ranking:

1. **Use "Question Title Tags"** (Question-based title tags have an above-average CTR).
2. **Fill In Missing Meta Descriptions** (Add in meta-descriptions for pages that need them).
3. **Use Review or FAQ Schema** (Using certain types of Schema can hook you up with Rich Snippets enhancing CTR).
4. **Add Some Emotion to Title Tags** (Write title tags with some emotion but avoid the portrayal as clickbaits).
5. **Add the Current Year to Title and Description** (Adding the year to title and description makes it clear that the content is up-to-date).

❖ **On-Page UX Signals**

In other words, how Google searchers interact with your content. Google's "How Search Works" says that, to help them rank the best results, they "use aggregated and anonymized interaction data to assess whether search results are relevant to queries".

1. **Push Content Above the Fold** (Content on the site must be direct and to the point).
2. **Chunk Your Content** (Make the content super easy to skim through by dividing into sections, heading, sub-heading and bullets etc.).
3. **Engage an Active Community** (It keeps people superglued to your site)

❖ **Advanced On-Page SEO Tips**

1. **Use Original Images** (Original and Unique images tend to have higher interaction).
2. **Do Internal Linking** (Internal Linking from high authority pages to low authority pages)
3. **Write Comprehensive Content** (Also, Use LSI Keywords - LSI keywords are synonyms that Google uses to determine a page's relevancy).
4. **Boost Your Page Speed** (It is one of the Google's Ranking Factors).
5. **Image Optimization** (Give every image on your site a descriptive filename and alt text - Alt text (alternative text), also known as "alt attributes", "alt descriptions", or technically incorrectly as "alt tags," are used within an HTML code to describe the appearance and function of an image on a page).
6. **Rank Your Content In Featured Snippets** (Huge increase in CTR)

Off-Page SEO

Off-page SEO is all about activities done off of a website, getting trust and authority signals from other websites to increase the site's search engine rankings. This mainly involves building high-quality backlinks to one's site.

➢ Google largely relies on Reputation Research, a site's off-site reputation to figure out whether or not that site can be trusted.

- **On-Page SEO vs. Off-Page SEO** (On-page SEO is everything that you can directly control on your website while Off-page SEO are actions that happen away from your website).
- **Boost Off-Page SEO With Backlinks**
  When it comes to off-page SEO, backlinks are super important. But, How?
    a. **Be a Data Source** (People didn't only link to the page because of "high quality content" but also to in reference to data and figures).
    b. **Double Down On Long-Form Content** (Long-form content gets 77% more links than shorter posts).
    c. **Strategic Guest Posting** (Build links from your guest posts, brand mentions etc.).
- **Generate Brand Signals**
  Signals that Google uses to figure out if any site is a legit brand or not.
    a. **Audit Your Branded Searches** (via Google Search Console, Branded searches are No. of people searching for your brand in Google).
    b. **Invest in YouTube** (YouTube marketing is one of the best ways to boost your site's Brand Signals).
    c. **Publish Research-Backed Content** (Research-backed content = high-quality links).
- **Improve E-A-T** (Expertise, Authoritativeness, Trustworthiness or Page Quality)
    a. **Get Brand Mentions on Authority Sites**
    b. **Get Links From Trusted "Seed Sites"** (Seed sites are the highly-trusted pages that search engines start crawls upon).
    c. **Get Positive Reviews Online** (Google's Quality Rater guidelines emphasizes online reviews).

Technical SEO

Google and other search engines can crawl and index all the pages on one's website. Technical SEO is the process of ensuring that a website meets the technical requirements of modern search engines with the goal of improved organic rankings. It includes things like crawling, indexing, rendering, making sure one's pages load quickly and that one's site architecture is set up correctly.

➢ The easier Google can access your content, the better the chance will be to rank. The site's pages need to be secure, mobile optimized, free of duplicate content, and fast-loading etc.

- **How to improve Technical SEO?**
  Take into account the following to improve Technical SEO:
  a. Javascript
  b. XML sitemaps
  c. Site architecture
  d. URL structure
  e. Structured data
  f. Thin content
  g. Duplicate content
  h. Hreflang
  i. Canonical tags
  j. 404 pages
  k. 301 redirects

- **Site Structure and Navigation**
  A strong site structure makes every other Technical SEO task much easier. The steps are:

  1. **Use a Flat, Organized Site Structure** (All the pages on the website must be organized, all pages be only a few links away from one another - search engines can then crawl 100% of site's pages.).
  2. **Consistent URL Structure** (URLs to follow a consistent, logical structure as pages under different categories gives Google extra context about each page in that category)
  3. **Breadcrumbs Navigation** (Breadcrumbs automatically add internal links to category and subpages on the site)

- **Crawling, Rendering and Indexing**
  1. **Spot Indexing Issues**

Find any pages on the site that search engine spiders have trouble crawling. 3 ways to do that:

    a) **Coverage Report** ("Coverage Report" in the Google Search Console, if Google is unable to fully index or render pages that must be indexed).

    b) **Screaming Frog** (Once issues are fixed in Coverage Report, running a full crawl with Screaming Frog is recommended).

    c) **Ahrefs Site Audit** (Audit your site with Ahrefs to get the information on the site's Technical SEO)

    d) **Internal Link to "Deep" Pages** (Strongly architecture your site to prevent the problems caused).

    e) **Use an XML Sitemap** (Google still needs a XML sitemap to find the website's URLs).

    f) **GSC "Inspect"** (A tool helps in identifying and solving the site's problems in indexing)

- **Thin and Duplicate Content**

  If there is Duplicate content present on the site originally or if the site's CMS created multiple versions of the same page on different URLs then it can hurt your overall site's rankings. So it's worth finding and fixing.

  How to fix?

  1. **Use Canonical URLs**

  A canonical URL is the URL of the page that Google thinks is most representative from a set of duplicate pages on the site. For example, if the site has URLs for the same page (for example: example.com?dress=1234 and example.com/dresses/1234), Google chooses one as canonical.

- **PageSpeed**

  Improving your pagespeed is one of the few technical SEO strategies that can directly impact the site's rankings. There are 3 simple ways to boost up the site's loading speed:

  1. **Reduce Web Page Size** (Page's total size correlated with load times, Compress images and cache the out of site).

  2. **Test Load Times With and Without a CDN** (CDNs are associated with worse load times).

  3. **Eliminate 3rd Party Scripts** (Each 3rd party script that a page adds an average of 34ms to its load time).

Country-Specific SEO

- ## How to target a specific country?

  The following is a basic checklist for targeting a specific country with international SEO:

  1. Use a country-specific domain.
  2. Specify the location you are targeting in Google Search Console.
  3. Register your business address with Google My Business.
  4. Include the street address of the business on the website.
  5. Host the website locally (as much for usability as for SEO).
  6. Get links from country-specific websites.
  7. Use the local language(s).

- ## Website Structure Choices for International SEO

  1. **Option 1: CCTLDs** (Country code top-level domain) is absolutely perfect for any businesses that are only considering targeting 2 or 3 countries – remember "countries" rather than languages – if you're aiming to target a language, *subdirectories* or *subfolders* are better.
  2. **Option 2: Subdomains** - http://**fr**.example.com.
  3. **Option 3: Subdirectories** - http://www.example.com/**fr**

- ## Technical Signals for International SEO

  1. **HrefLang Tags** gives your content a global SEO boost. Use hreflang for these two reasons:
     i. *For a better user experience.* Content created specifically for an audience and delivered in their own language will resonate, engage and meet the user search expectation. This leads to a lower bounce rate and better page rankings.
     ii. *To prevent duplicate content issues.* If you have pages with the same content in different languages or regionally-specific content in the same language, Google might not understand and see it as duplicate content, which can impact page ranking. Like canonical tags, hreflang helps to avoid penalties associated with duplicate content across global sites.
  2. **Canonical Tag** (aka "rel canonical") is a way of telling search engines that a specific URL represents the master copy of a page. Using the canonical tag prevents problems caused by identical or **"duplicate" content** appearing on multiple URLs.
  3. **X Default Tag** is basically a default version of the site that you can choose to be served to people when the language or location tag doesn't match any of the available ones and no other page is better suited. So say you have a UK and US version of the site, but someone from Australia searches for related terms – you'd xdefault them to a preferred version.
  4. **Meta Content Language Tags** indicates what language the html content is written in (and can include country too), and therefore signals to search engines the target audience for the page. This is a much weaker signal than hreflang tags.

5. **Schema Markup** is a very simple and effective method for indicating to search engines what your website is about, and what your company does. It's a collaboratively created, universal language that all top search engines in the world use to understand websites easily – you may have heard of it referred to as structured data, a hot topic in SEO at the minute. *You can add schema markup with *Google Tag Manager*.

❖ **Create a sitemap**
❖ **Change content based on local culture**
❖ **International Link Building**

1. Local citation building
2. General and competitor research
3. Use tools such as BuzzSumo to discover what topics and types of content work best in your target market (also helpful for competitor research).

Google's 8 Most Important Ranking Factors (2021)

Google's Ranking Factors are the factors upon which Google judges and then ranks the websites in SERPs. SEO community almost always try to get hold of some new ranking factors, here is a list of 200 Google ranking factors, each of which can make or break your search optimization strategy for 2021.

The most important Google ranking factors in 2021 are:

1. Referring domains

2. Organic click-through-rate

3. Domain authority

4. Mobile usability

5. Dwell time

6. Total number of backlinks

7. Content quality

8. On-page SEO

Bonus: SEO in 2021

❖ **Core Web Vitals:**

Core web vitals are a set of three specific web page experience metrics that Google considers super important:

- Largest Contentful Paint
- First Input Delay
- Cumulative Layout Shift

The aforementioned Core Web Vitals are part of Google's overall evaluation of "page experience". According to Google, core web vitals will directly impact rankings.

1. **Largest Contentful Paint (LCP)**

   LCP is a Core Web Vitals metric and measures when the largest content element in the viewport becomes visible. It can be used to determine when the main content of the page has finished rendering on the screen. The most common causes of a poor LCP are: Slow server response times.

2. **First Input Delay (FID)**

   FID measures the time from when a user first interacts with your site (i.e. when they click a link, tap on a button, or use a custom, JavaScript-powered control) to the time when the browser is actually able to respond to that interaction.

3. **Cumulative Layout Shift (CLS)**

   CLS is the unexpected shifting of web page elements while the page is still downloading. The kinds of elements that tend to cause shift are fonts, images, videos, contact forms, buttons and other kinds of content.

❖ **Google Passages Ranking:**

Google passage indexing is an automated feature that pulls sections from pages into search engine results.

- Passages allow Google to rank specific, relevant passages from a specific page. Not just the page itself. (Page section relevance rather than the entire page relevance).
- Backlinks, on-page SEO, UX signals, and Google's other page-level ranking factors will still apply.
- **How to Optimize for Passages?**

1. Organize content into discrete sections.
2. Double Down on *Long Form Content*

❖ **Featured Snippets:**

Featured Snippets are short snippets of text that appear at the top of Google's search results in order to quickly answer a searcher's query. The content that appears inside of a Featured Snippet is automatically pulled from web pages in Google's index. Common types of Featured Snippets include definitions, tables, steps and lists.

- **How to Optimize for Featured Snippets?**
  1. Find Featured Snippet opportunities. (Keyword Research + Featured Snippets are from the pages who already rank on the first page)
  2. *Snippet Bait* (A snippet bait is a 40-60 word block placed at the beginning of an article. It makes it easier for Google to pull up a summary from your article to show it to users).
  3. Content formatting for all types of Featured Snippets. i.e.
     a) Paragraph snippets (Most common)
     b) Numbered list snippets
     c) Bulleted list snippets
     d) Table snippets

❖ **Visual Search:**

Visual search is an artificial intelligence technology that allows users to conduct an internet search using a picture, rather than keywords.

- Bing Visual Search, Google Lense, Tineye = *Visual Search Engines*.
- **How to Optimize for Visual Search?**
  1. Design Mobile-Friendly Pages
  2. Carry on the Traditional Image SEO
  3. Creaete Content-Rich Pages (1600 words on average).

❖ **Domain Authority:**

The domain authority of a website describes its relevance for a specific subject area or industry. This relevance has a direct impact on its ranking by search engines, trying to assess domain authority through automated analytic algorithms.

- Google evaluates sites based on Expertise, Authoritativeness, and Trustworthiness (EAT).
- **How to establish EAT?**
  1. Be an Expert as Google wants to feature content that's written by legit experts in their field.
  2. Be Transparent. i.e.

→ Thorough "about" page.

→ Easy to find "contact" page.

→ References and external links to sources.

→ Privacy policy and terms of service.

→ Author bylines on every article.

3. Be Cited (Social Media mentions, sites referrals, rankings etc)

❖ **Video Content:**

A video rich snippet means that when someone searches for something on Google, you can have a small tiny video show up next to your result to let the user know that particular result (yours) has a video to help.

- **How to create a Video Featured Snippets?**
  1. Organize Your Content Into Discrete Sections

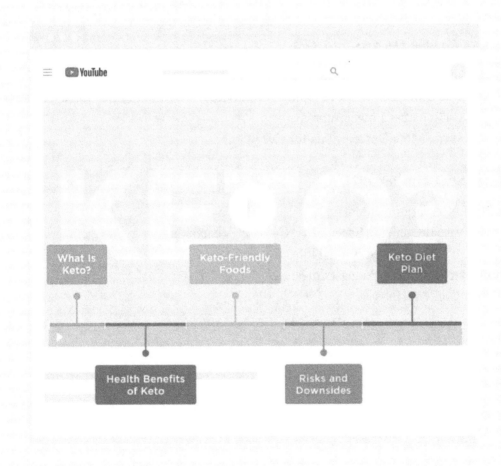

  2. Video SEO Optimization (title, description and tags).
  3. Provide a Transcript (Captions).
- Grow Your YouTube Channel

- Embed Video Content Into Text-Based Blog Posts (Decreases Bounce Rate)

❖ **Master Search Intent**

Search intent is the reason behind a searcher's query on search engines. It represents the objective the searcher is trying to accomplish. For example, someone might want to learn about something, find something, or buy something.

- **How to Master Search Intent?**

  1. Identify Each Keyword's Intent
  2. Create Content That's a 1:1 Search Intent Match
  3. Re-Optimize Old Content for Search Intent

❖ **Combat Decreasing CTRs**

In the SERPs, your result needs to scream "click on me!"… or else it'll be ignored.

- *How to Combat Decreasing CTRs*

  1. Include Your Keyword in Your URL
  2. Use Emotion (Without Going Overboard) - emotional titles have a relatively high CTR.+ Less Power Words
  3. Write Meta Descriptions for Every Page

❖ **Quick SEO Tips for 2021**

1. Publish "Research Content"
2. Create Visual Content (Especially "Concept Visuals")
3. Optimize Your Podcast Show Notes for SEO
4. Build Backlinks as a Podcast Guest
5. Publish Content Hubs

References

Author, G., McCormick, K., Whitney, M., Bond, C., & Donnelly, G. (2020, September 09). *The wordstream blog*. Retrieved March 13, 2021, from https://www.wordstream.com/blog?category=109&author=All&page=1

Dean, B. (2020, December 16). *SEO in 2021: The Definitive Guide*. Retrieved March 13, 2021, from https://backlinko.com/seo-this-year

Dean, B. (n.d.). *SEO fundamentals*. Retrieved March 13, 2021, from https://backlinko.com/hub/seo/fundamentals

Dean, B. (2021, February 17). *What is SEO? Search engine optimization in plain English*. Retrieved March 13, 2021, from https://backlinko.com/hub/seo/what-is-seo

Google search. (n.d.). Retrieved March 13, 2021, from https://www.google.com/search/howsearchworks/algorithms/

German, T. (2020, May 27). *SEO Basics: The Uncomplicated Guide to Simplifying SEO*. Retrieved March 13, 2021, from https://www.seoclarity.net/resources/knowledgebase/seo-basics-guide-to-simplifying-seo

Google. (n.d.). Retrieved March 13, 2021, from https://developers.google.com/search/docs/beginner/seo-starter-guide?hl=en&visit_id=637442370133919859-1334767259&rd=1

Google SEO 2021: COMPLETE SEO beginner's guide. (2021, February 05). Retrieved March 13, 2021, from https://backlinko.com/google-seo-guide

Keyword research for SEO: The Definitive Guide (2021 Update). (2020, October 13). Retrieved March 13, 2021, from https://backlinko.com/keyword-research

Search engine positioning. (2020, October 28). Retrieved March 13, 2021, from https://backlinko.com/hub/seo/search-engine-positioning

SEO best PRACTICES: 10 tips to improve your Google rankings. (2020, December 28). Retrieved March 13, 2021, from https://backlinko.com/hub/seo/best-practices

What are short tail keywords for SEO? (+ real examples). (2021, March 03). Retrieved March 13, 2021, from https://loganix.com/short-tail-keywords/#:~:text=Short%20tail%20keywords%20are%20search,of%20a%20long%20tail%20keyword.

www.ingramcontent.com/pod-product-compliance
Lightning Source LLC
LaVergne TN
LVHW081807050326
832903LV00027B/2131